access

3

DAS FERIENHEFT

A holiday language course with Merit and Onno

Vokabeltrainer-App

Verfügbar für: iOS, Android und Windows Phone

 Deine Audios **findest du hier:**

1. Melde dich auf scook.de an.
2. Gib den unten stehenden Zugangscode in die Box ein.
3. Hab viel Spaß mit den Audios.

Dein Zugangscode auf
www.scook.de

Die Audios können dort nach Bestätigung der AGB und Lizenzbedingungen genutzt werden.

ybbxr-vs2ef

Cornelsen

English G Access · Band 3

DAS FERIENHEFT

A holiday language course with Merit and Onno

Herausgeber
Prof. Jörg Rademacher, Mannheim

Erarbeitet von
Dr. Angelika Thiele, Münster

Redaktion
Stefan Höhne (Projektleitung);
Ulrike Berendt, Priscilla Lavodrama

Illustrationen
Christian Bartz, Berlin

Umschlagfoto
mauritius images, Mittenwald (Big Ben (M):
ImageBROKER); plainpicture GmbH, Hamburg
(The Shard (M): Ableimages/David Harrigan)

Umschlaggestaltung
kleiner & bold, Berlin
hawemannundmosch, Berlin
klein & halm Grafikdesign, Berlin

Layoutkonzept
Yvonne Thron (designcollective), Berlin

Technische Umsetzung
Petra Eberhard (designcollective), Berlin

Soweit in diesem Lehrwerk Personen fotografisch abgebildet sind und ihnen von der Redaktion fiktive Namen, Berufe, Dialoge und Ähnliches zugeordnet oder diese Personen in bestimmte Kontexte gesetzt werden, dienen diese Zuordnungen und Darstellungen ausschließlich der Veranschaulichung und dem besseren Verständnis des Lehrwerksinhalts.

Tonaufnahmen
Studio: Clarity Studio, Berlin
Regie und Aufnahmeleitung: Christian Schmitz, Berlin
Tontechnik: Christian Schmitz; Pascal Thinius

www.cornelsen.de

Die Webseiten Dritter, deren Internetadressen in diesem Lehrwerk angegeben sind, wurden vor Drucklegung sorgfältig geprüft. Der Verlag übernimmt keine Gewähr für die Aktualität und den Inhalt dieser Seiten oder solcher, die mit ihnen verlinkt sind.

1. Auflage, 3. Druck 2021

Alle Drucke dieser Auflage sind inhaltlich unverändert und können im Unterricht nebeneinander verwendet werden.

Druck: Athesiadruck GmbH

ISBN: 978-3-06-033636-4

PEFC zertifiziert
Dieses Produkt stammt aus nachhaltig bewirtschafteten Wäldern und kontrollierten Quellen.

www.pefc.de

PEFC/18-31-166

Liebe Schülerin, lieber Schüler,

endlich Ferien! Zeit, um sich zu erholen, alte Freunde zu treffen und neue kennenzulernen.

Doch ein entspannter Start in Klasse 8 ist ebenso wichtig. Das gelingt dir am besten, wenn du den Stoff aus Klasse 7 wiederholst. Dieses Heft, in dem du die Bekanntschaft von Merit und Onno machst, hilft dir dabei, Wortschatz und Grammatik zu festigen. In abwechslungsreichen und manchmal auch kniffligen Übungen kannst du lesen, hören und deine Aussprache schulen.

Natürlich gibt es auch einen Lösungsteil. Er beginnt auf Seite 43. Blättere jedoch nicht gleich nach hinten, wenn du nicht weiter weißt. Manchmal musst du nur ein bisschen knobeln, um auf die Lösung zu kommen.

And now have fun with Merit and Onno!

Deine Englischredaktion

1 This is England!

Sky-blue, purple and pink. Nice colours – for some, but not for 13-year-old Onno. He was sitting on a pink bed in a VERY small room with two sky-blue and two purple walls, somewhere in Richmond in south-west London, looking stressed and unhappy. His parents! How could they send him to England in his holidays to stay with this strange family? His English was quite good – well, it wasn't SO bad. As he was thinking of his parents, he remembered something; Mum had asked him to give her a ring as soon as he arrived at the Wrights'. Onno moved off the bed, opened his rucksack and looked for his smartphone. Empty! Of course! He knew it. That battery was awful, rubbish. It didn't even keep for 12 hours.

So electricity was needed again. Onno tried hard to put the plug[1] into one of those funny white things on the wall, but they had three square holes, not two round ones as in Germany. It just wouldn't go in. Onno was in shock! His smartphone, his notebook – nothing would work now. A loud knock on the door brought Onno back into the blue, purple and pink world of a Richmond family house. 'Dinner is ready. Are you coming down?'

When Onno came into the big dining room, an old lady and two kids were already sitting at a huge dinner table. 'This is 'O' …, er, this is 'Ohno' from Germany, Mother. He'll be with us for three weeks. He's doing one of the language courses at a college in Roehampton,' said Mrs Wright to the old lady. 'Oh, lovely, lovely,' the old lady answered in an even older voice. Before Onno could decide if he had to shake hands with anybody, Mrs Wright took him by the shoulder and pushed him softly to an empty chair next to two teenage girls. 'This is Hannah and here is Kayla.' Mrs Wright pointed to her two daughters. 'Hi!' – 'Hi!' – 'Hi!' Onno was quite happy with how the 'hi' had come out of his mouth. Ah, good, there was Dexter, Hannah and Kayla's younger brother. The two boys had already been in email contact. 'Hi,' Dexter said and sat down next to Onno. 'I was looking for Macy's dog food. Is there any left?' he asked his mother. 'I don't know,' she answered. 'Let's eat now. The fish stew is getting cold.' Fish? Onno felt another shock in his stomach while his head was quickly going through all the English words that he knew. The word 'vegetarian[2]' was not one of them.

---

[1] plug [plʌg] *Stecker* [2] vegetarian [ˌvedʒɪˈteərɪən] *Vegetarier*

a) Read the text on the left. Who's who? Write the names next to the numbers.

1 _____ 2 _____ 3 _____

4 *Kayla* _____

6 _____

7 _____   5 _____

b) Are the sentences right or wrong, or is the information not in the text?
Mark a letter.

		Right	Wrong	Not in the text
1	Onno is twelve years old.	H	M	F
2	Dexter is younger than Onno.	A	C	R
3	Onno doesn't like fish.	U	N	L
4	Onno is going to go to a language school in England.	A	W	O
5	Mrs Wright's mother and Onno shook hands.	D	H	V
6	Onno's mum tried to phone the Wrights.	L	E	B
7	Six people had dinner in the evening.	G	R	O

If your answers are right, you will have the letters which make up the name of the city where Onno comes from. Just put them in the right order.

Onno is from _____ .

2 It's a dog's life!

Read the text, look at the words on the right and choose the right word for each gap.

'Believe it or not, I'm hungry again. People say I've got a good (1) _____ . Of course, I have. You need to eat, or you won't survive. My favourite food is (2) _____ , hamburgers, sausages, etc. But I don't like it if it's too (3) _____ . Once they gave me meat with a lot of chilli and cayenne pepper! That was really horrible[1], I can tell you. No, I like it nice and (4) _____ . You have to be careful if you get something from an Indian restaurant or from an Indian (5) _____ . Indian (6) _____ can be very, very spicy. I don't really need (7) _____ , just give me something dry and I'm happy. If there's no time to prepare it, I'll have it (8) _____ . No problem. I eat fish too, if I have to. There's that fish which looks pink when it's cooked – that's OK for me. I think they call it (9) '_____' – with a silent 'l'. What I really hate is (10) _____ of any colour, orange, red or green: carrots, tomatoes or lettuce[2]. And I can't stand those small brown things called (11) _____ either. And the one thing I'm (12) _____ to is onions. One onion alone could kill me if I ate it. But it seems that I'm going to die of hunger first anyway. It's a dog's life!'

[1] horrible ['hɒrəbl] *schrecklich*   [2] lettuce ['letɪs] *Salat*

3 Talking about transport

a) Add the correct verbs (plus preposition) to the mindmaps.

arrive at • go by • take • get off • change to • walk ✔

to school   to the bus stop

1 *walk* _____

home

the Northern Line   platform 7

2 _____

the underground

the underground

a ride

3 _____

the bus   a taxi

taxi   bike

plane

4 _____

car   boat

the bus   at the next stop

here

5 _____

the train   your bike

the airport   the station

work   6 _____   school

a friend's house

b) Find and match two words that make a new word or which belong together as two words.

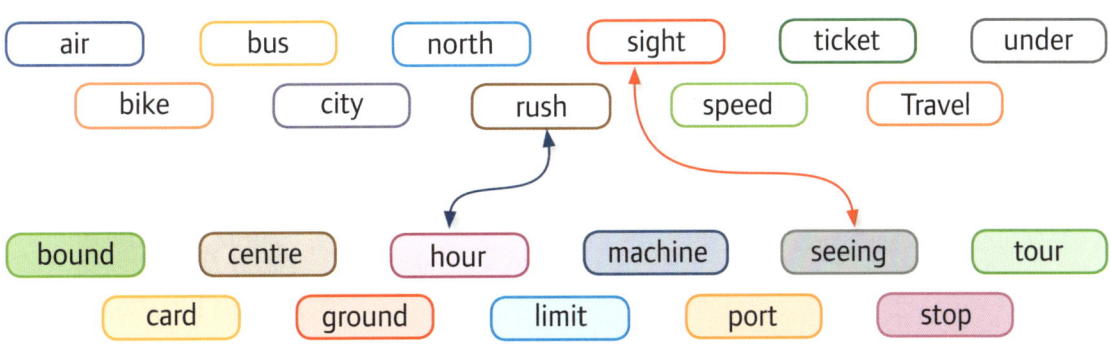

air   bus   north   sight   ticket   under

bike   city   rush   speed   Travel

bound   centre   hour   machine   seeing   tour

card   ground   limit   port   stop

One word: *sightseeing,* _____

Two words: *rush hour,* _____

4 An email for Onno (Simple past, present perfect)

A few months before his trip to London, Onno got this email from his host family's son, Dexter. Complete the text with the verbs in brackets ( ).

Dear Onno,

Hi, I'm Dexter. Yesterday we (1) _____ (get) a letter from the language

school that you are going to this summer. They (2) _____ (tell) us that

you're going to stay with us for three weeks in August. That's cool!

(3) _____ you _____ (be) to England before?

I (4) _____ (never be) to Germany, but I (5) _____ (go)

skiing[1] with my family in the Austrian Alps last winter. My German isn't very good,

I (6) _____ (have) German lessons for two years now. As you might

know, we live in Richmond, London. We (7) _____ (move) here four

years ago. What else? I'm mad about football! My club is ManU (that's short for

Manchester United), and I (8) _____ (already, be) to

Old Trafford (that's their stadium) three times. Two weeks ago they (9)

_____ (play) against FC Chelsea here in London and (10) _____

(beat) them 2–0! What about you, Onno? What kind of person are you ;-)? Write

back soon. I'm looking forward to seeing you this summer!

Yours,

Dexter

[1] ski [ski:] *Ski fahren*

5 Asking the way 🎧

a) 🔊 Onno is taking the Wrights' dog for a walk. Listen to the sound file. Then <mark>mark</mark> the correct answers.

1   The Wrights' house is at …
- T 22 Lewis Street.
- S 24 Lewis Road.
- L Evelyn Road.

2   The old lady thinks Macy is …
- E a good name for a dog.
- A not a King Charles Spaniel.
- H not the best name for this dog.

3   The lady who helps Onno says that Germany is …
- V OK.
- E beautiful.
- W nice.

4   Which big building is near the Wrights' house?
- E the Odeon cinema
- O a museum
- I a shopping mall

5   Check the map: At which point is Onno when he meets the friendly lady?
- R 1
- N 2
- S 3
- Y 4

If your answers are right, the letters make the name of a road in Richmond.
It's _____ Road.

b) 🔊 The friendly lady explains to Onno how to get home. Use the map in order to find the way and put her explanations in the right order. But the lady makes one mistake (she gets 'left' and 'right' wrong). Can you find this mistake? Correct it.

	Walk along Red Lion Street for a few minutes, and the Odeon is on the left side of the street.
	At the end of Eton Street, turn left into Red Lion Street.
1	Well, first of all you walk down Evelyn Road till you come to George Street.
	Turn left into Eton Street.
	Turn right there, go along George Street, past the big shopping mall.

6 Some facts about the Wright family (Simple past, present perfect)

Use the information in the table in order to write some sentences about the Wrights.

Who?		What?	(Since) when?
1		sing in the Richmond Choir	last summer
2		work as a pilot	for 15 years
3		be married	since June 23rd, 1994
4		be on Facebook	since 15th birthday

Who?		What?	(Since) when?
5		keep a diary	for six months
6		date her boyfriend Ben	last week
7		live in Richmond	for 45 years
8		catch three mice[1]	last April

[1] mice (pl.) [maɪs] Mäuse

1 Mrs Wright sang in the Richmond Choir last summer.

2 Mr Wright _____ .

3 _____ .

4 _____ .

5 _____ .

6 _____ .

7 _____ .

8 _____ .

7 Oh! Ouch! The sounds [əʊ] and [aʊ] 🎧

Underline every word which has an [əʊ] sound, as in *nobody* for example, and circle every word that as an [aʊ] sound, as in under(ground). After you have done this, you can listen to the words on the sound file.

1 around the table

2 the house in Richmond

3 cool sound

4 you know

5 foul play

6 below zero

7 a sore throat

8 a cold shower

9 Oh no!

10 touch ground

11 not now

12 south-west London

13 our own clothes

14 loud laughter

8 What has been happening? (Present perfect progressive)

It is 11 pm at the Wrights' house. Read the example and then complete the sentences.

1 The dog is sleeping on Dexter's bed. It jumped onto the bed at 9 pm.

   The dog has been sleeping for two hours.

2 Mrs Wright is watching her favourite programme on TV. She turned the TV on at 10.30.

   She _____ half an hour.

3 Kayla is talking to her best friend on the phone. Her friend called her at 8.30.

   Kayla _____ .

4 Hannah is doing her hair. It was 10 o'clock when she began.

   Hannah _____ .

5 Grandma is doing a crossword puzzle in the armchair. She wrote the first word at 9.30.

   Grandma _____ .

6 Dexter is listening to his MP3 player. He put his headphones on at 9.45.

   Dexter _____ .

7 And where is Mr Wright? Well, he's flying across the Atlantic. He's a pilot and his plane left

   Ontario airport at 8 o'clock British summer time.

   Mr Wright _____ .

9 Wimbledon – here I am

'In Wimbledon!! Yesss!!!' Merit tapped 'Post' on her smartphone and a few seconds later her 748 friends on a famous social networking service got the information that she had arrived safely at the family she was staying with in Wimbledon in south-west London – those that were online at least. Merit's parents wanted her to improve her English and had sent her to London for a three-week English course. She was staying with a family, the Richardsons. Mr Richardson had just picked her up from the airport. Now she was relaxing after the journey in one of the rooms at the top of the Richardsons' house, right under the roof.

Merit didn't really have time to look around her room because she was busy reading the answers that were coming in on her smartphone. She didn't care either. Not even about the huge crowd of teddy bears in all colours, shapes and sizes that were sitting around her

on the bed. She was so busy that she didn't even hear a little girl come in the door. 'This is my room,' the little girl grumbled[1] to Merit in a loud and angry voice. 'Aargh! Ouch!' Merit jumped up in shock and surprise and hit her head on the wall over her bed. The girl laughed out loud, then she got angry again. 'You're sitting on my teddies. This is my room! And my bed!' Although Merit was not a shy girl – far from it – this little monster of a girl almost made her forget her English. Almost, but not quite: 'Eh? Who are you?', she said, puzzled[2] and holding her head. The little monster answered with a hard kick against her – and Merit's – bed, so hard that two teddies in red and pink T-shirts fell off it – plonk, plonk!

Luckily, at that moment Mr Richardson looked through the door. 'Jessie! What are you doing here? Let Merit unpack her bags. By the way, Merit, have you met Jessie? She's going to sleep in her little brother's room while you're here. Ah, and this is Pierre from Orléans in France.' A boy's head with a big smile appeared from behind Mr Richardson's arm. 'Pierre is staying with us for the next three weeks too.' 'Aha … ohooo', Merit thought, but she didn't say anything, of course. 'Pierre, this is Merit from Germany,' Mr Richardson went on. 'You two will be going to the same language school in Roehampton. And you'll meet Merit's brother Onno there too. He's going to do the English course with you, but he's staying with another family. That way they won't speak German to each other all the time.'

Suddenly a terrible noise came up the stairs, as if the kitchen cupboard with all the plates and pots and things had fallen down. 'Oh dear!' Mr Richardson sounded worried. 'Jessie, come on, let's help your mum in the kitchen. She's got a big cooking job tonight.' 'A big cooking job?' Merit thought to herself. 'Just because Pierre and me are here? How strange!'

---

[1] grumble ['grʌmbl] *meckern* [2] puzzled ['pʌzld] *verwirrt*

Read the text on the left. What does it tell you about Merit? Complete the sentences about her.

1 Merit is staying with _a family_ in Wimbledon.

2 She has _____ frie_____ on a _____.

3 She must im_____ , her par_____ say.

4 She came to _____ by pla_____.

5 She has one of _____ under the _____.

6 She isn't a _____ girl.

7 She is puzzled because she _____ the little girl is.

8 She seems to like _____ .

10 If A, then B (Conditional I)

Fill in the right form of the verbs.

1 If Merit works harder for English, she (1) _'ll get_
   (get) better results in her English tests.

2 If she (2) _gets_ better results in her English tests, her mother (3) _____
   (be) happier.

3 If her mother (4) _____ happier, she (5) _____
   (not grumble) so much.

4 If she (6) _____ so much, Merit (7) _____
   (not have) so many arguments with her.

5 If she (8) _____ so many arguments with her, it (9) _____
   (be) much nicer at home.

6 If it (10) _____ much nicer at home, Merit's friends (11) _____

   _____ (come and visit) her more often.

11 In town

Find an expression which fits the definition and put it in the line with the same number. All the parts of the expressions are in mirror writing in the box below.

1 A place where people can watch others doing sport, for example playing football.

2 Usually the most important city in a country.

3 You can leave your car here.

4 A round, open place in a town where a few streets meet, for example London's Picc…

5 It's tall, round and made of stone.

6 A church is for Christians. This building is for Muslims.

7 It's a place for talking and making laws.

8 An open area, usually with four sides and buildings around it.

9 A building where neighbours can meet.

10 A huge building where you can buy almost everything and where you can eat and drink.

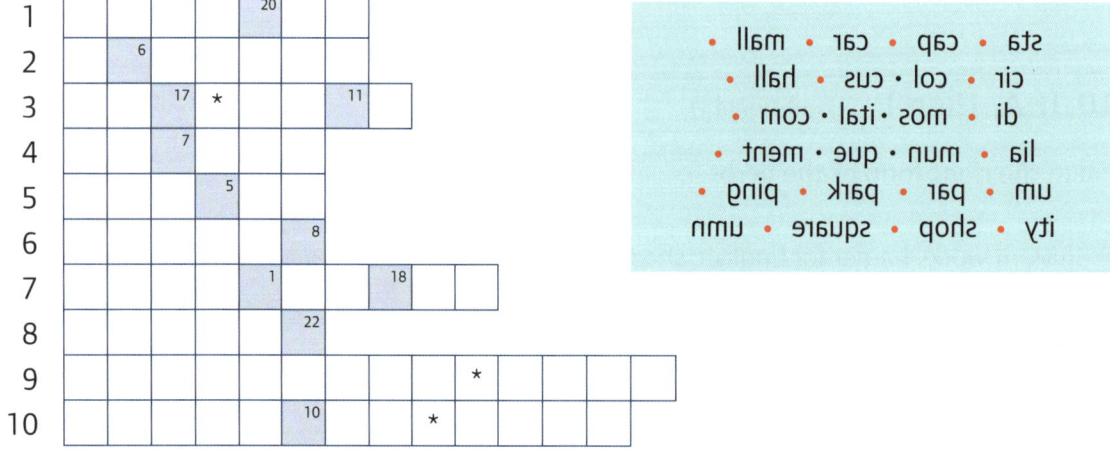

The letters in the blue boxes with numbers can be used to complete the sentence.

__ F YO __ __ __ __ T __ __ ED OF LONDON,
1   5   6 7 8   10 11

YOU A __ __ TIRED OF L __ F __.
        17 18   20   22

(Samuel Johnson, 1709 – 1784, English writer)

12 A trip to the Science Museum

Dexter had to write a report on a school trip. Which words in the boxes can replace[1] the boring words *nice* and *and*? Put the number that you see in the text before the word in the box. Then write down the correct words from the boxes.

clear and useful words for 'and'

____ : although	____ : because
____ : but	____ : so
____ : when	____ : where

more interesting words for 'nice'

____ 40-minute	____ : best
1 : famous	____ : impressive[2]
____ : large	____ : old

On 3rd June our class visited the (1) ~~nice~~ *famous* Science Museum in London. After a

(2) ~~nice~~ _____ ride on the tube, we finally arrived there at 10 am. When I first

saw the museum, I thought 'wow' this building is very (3) ~~nice~~ _____ . We had a

lot of time to look at it (4) ~~and~~ _____ we had to wait ten minutes to get in.

Believe me, I'm not a real museum lover, (5) ~~and~~ _____ this is such an exciting

place! There are more than 300,000 (!) objects in the museum (6) ~~and~~ _____

I can't list them all here. I loved the rooms with the (7) ~~nice~~ _____ railway[3]

trains most of all. I saw a locomotive from 1829! There is also a (8) ~~nice~~ _____

museum shop (9) ~~and~~ _____ they sell lots of things, like posters, pens,

books, models and games. Some of us wanted to buy souvenirs in the museum shop, but we

didn't have enough time. We were all sad to leave (10) ~~and~~ _____

the museum closed at 6 pm. Even my (11) ~~nice~~ _____ friend Dave liked it

(12) ~~and~~ _____ he usually hates museums.

If you put the words in the boxes in the right order (from 1–12), the marked letters will give you the name of a famous object in the Science Museum.

It's the _____ .

[1] replace [rɪ'pleɪs] *ersetzen*   [2] impressive [ɪm'presɪv] *beeindruckend*   [3] railway ['reɪlweɪ] *Eisenbahn*

13 In and out of London – Guess What 🎧

a) Before you listen, match the place names with the photos. Try and guess if you don't know. Write the letter in the box on the photo.

A	Buckingham Palace
B	British Museum
C	The Old Man of Hoy
D	Tower Bridge
E	Eiffel Tower
F	St Paul's Cathedral
G	Stanley Park
H	Covent Garden
I	Big Ben
J	Trafalgar Square[1]
K	The London Eye
L	Harrods[2]

1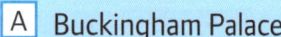
2
3
4
5
6
7
8
9
10
11
12
13

b) 👆 Listen to the sound file and see if you got the correct answers. Then play the 'Guess What' game: The speaker will think of one photo and tell you something about it. Put a cross (✗) under the photos that don't fit[3] the speaker's description until there's only one photo left. That's the photo the speaker was thinking of.

Photo ▶ Game ▼	1	2	3	4	5	6	7	8	9	10	11	12
1		✗										
2												
3												

1 admiral [ˈædmərəl] *Admiral* 2 department store [dɪˈpɑːtmənt stɔː(r)] *Kaufhaus* 3 fit [fɪt] *passen*

14 Clever or unclever?

a) You can change the meaning of these words with one of the prefixes *un-*, *im-*, *in-*, *ir-* or *dis-*. Write down these words with the correct prefix.

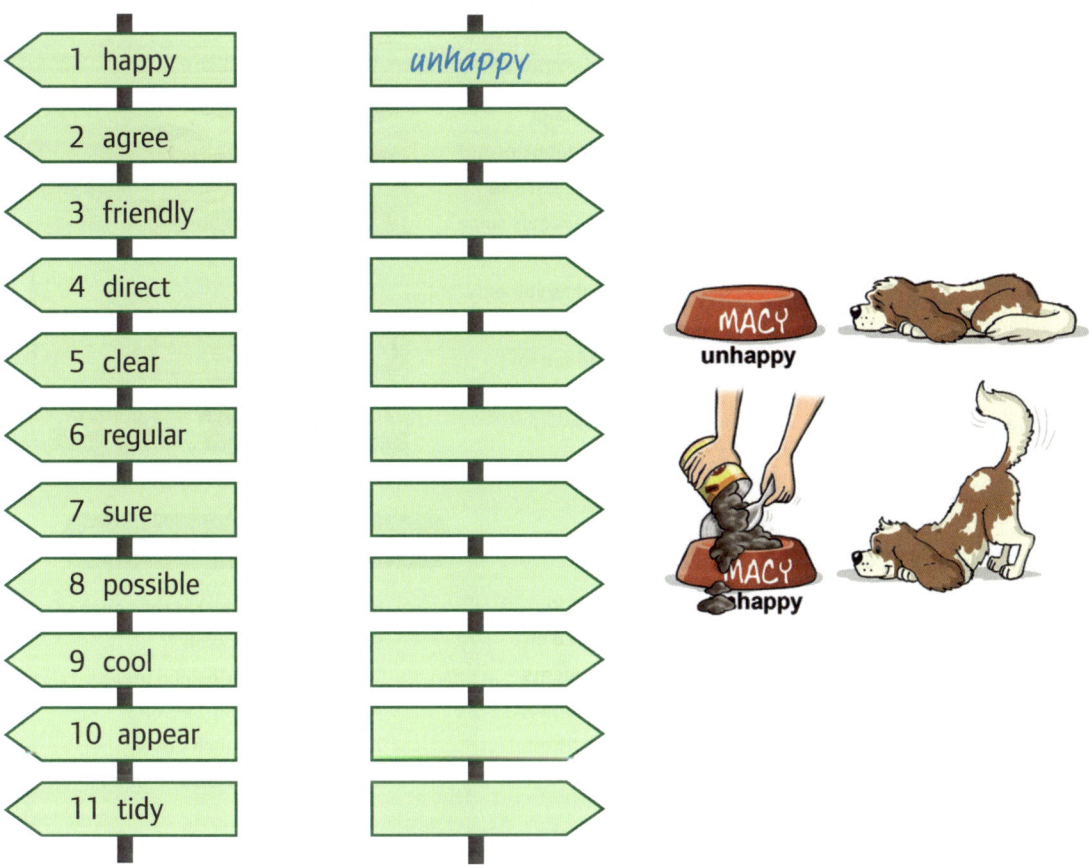

1 happy — *unhappy*

2 agree

3 friendly

4 direct

5 clear

6 regular

7 sure

8 possible

9 cool

10 appear

11 tidy

MACY unhappy

MACY happy

b) Find seven more adjectives that can take the prefix *un-*. Mark them. Then write down the adjectives with *un-*.

M	I	R	C	L	E	N	P	C
S	T	L	U	C	K	Y	N	O
N	E	X	E	L	Y	R	T	M
Y	E	S	N	E	I	N	I	F
F	O	P	L	V	M	R	E	O
A	S	O	W	E	S	H	O	R
I	M	P	O	R	T	A	N	T
R	E	U	N	E	P	P	S	A
S	I	L	U	T	R	P	N	B
N	S	A	F	E	M	Y	L	L
Y	E	R	T	C	T	N	S	E

1 *unfair*　　　　5 _____

2 _____　　　　6 _____

3 _____　　　　7 _____

4 _____　　　　8 _____

15 A college website

Junior Language College Roehampton

Learn English for Life!

Languages:

Welcome to Junior Language College Roehampton! My name is Adam Johnson and I'm the head teacher of the college. We've offered language courses for teenagers since 1992. Our school is in a nice, quiet area in the south-west of London, and it takes you only 20 minutes by tube to get to the heart of London. You'll like it – come and see for yourself!

Adam Johnson – Head Teacher

- Home
- Meet the team
- About Roehampton
- About our school
- Prices for all courses
- Test your English

Where you stay

You stay with real Londoners in their families or – if you are 18 or over – in flats with other students – but always close to our school. You can walk or take a bus – it'll never take longer than 15 minutes to get there. We promise!

What a typical school day is like

- 8.30 – 9 am: Arrival at the college
- 9 – 10.30 am: Lesson 1
- 10.30 – 11 am: Morning break
- 11 am – 12.30 pm: Lesson 2
- 12.30 – 2 pm: Lunch break
- 2 – 3.30 pm: Lesson 3

Free-time activities

Choose from different activities in the afternoon, for example: shopping, exploring London, doing sports, talking to Londoners, relaxing in Richmond Park …

Our special 3-week summer course for teenagers

- 15 lessons (90 minutes each) per week
- 2 different teachers per class, both from the UK
- maximum of 12 students per class
- a sightseeing trip every Wednesday
- project work (London Underground, fashion, football clubs in London …)
- £1900 all-inclusive

Contact us:
Facebook
Email
Telephone

On the left, you can see the website of the Junior Language College Roehampton, where Merit and Onno are doing their summer language course. Read it and find the answers to the questions below. Tick (✔) the right box and give short answers. Try to find the answers as quickly as you can.

1 How long is the trip from the Language College to the centre of London if you take the tube?

☐ 15 minutes ☐ 18 minutes ☐ 20 minutes ☐ 30 minutes

2 Roehampton is in ..?.. London.

☐ south-west ☐ south-east ☐ north-west ☐ north-east

3 How long is a lesson at the college?

☐ 45 minutes ☐ 60 minutes ☐ 75 minutes ☐ 90 minutes

4 Junior Language College Roehampton has offered language courses for teenagers for more than

☐ 10 years. ☐ 20 years. ☐ 30 years. ☐ 40 years.

5 How many different ways are there for people to contact the college?

☐ 1 ☐ 2 ☐ 3 ☐ 4

6 All the teachers of the 3-week summer course are from

☐ the UK. ☐ Germany. ☐ the USA. ☐ London.

7 What is the motto of the college?

_____

8 Who is Adam Johnson?

_____

9 When does a typical school day end at the college?

_____

10 How much does the 3-week summer course cost?

_____

11 If you want to find out how good your English is, click on …

_____

12 After finishing their 3-week summer course, the students will have had _____ lessons.

16 More about Merit (Conditional I)

On the second day at the college, Merit has to write a short text about her expectations towards the language programme. Fill in the right form of the verbs.

1 If I (1) _____ (not speak) German with Onno that much,

   I (2) _____ (learn) more English words.

2 I (3) _____ (improve) very quickly if I (4) _____ (take)
   15 English lessons per week.

3 I (5) _____ (can) turn to two teachers if I (6) _____ (have)
   a question.

4 If I (7) _____ (struggle[1]) with my homework, I (8) _____ (ask)
   my host mother for help.

5 I (9) _____ (learn) French too if Pierre (10) _____ (teach)
   me some words.

17 Stress in words 🎧

Read the words in the box. Is the stress on the first, second or third syllable of the word? Write the words in the table, then listen and check.

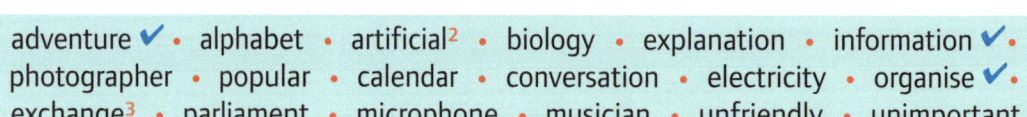

adventure ✔ · alphabet · artificial[2] · biology · explanation · information ✔·
photographer · popular · calendar · conversation · electricity · organise ✔·
exchange[3] · parliament · microphone · musician · unfriendly · unimportant

Stress on the first syllable:	Stress on the second syllable:	Stress on the third syllable:
1 _organise_	1 _adventure_	1 _information_
2 _____	2 _____	2 _____
3 _____	3 _____	3 _____
4 _____	4 _____	4 _____
5 _____	5 _____	5 _____
6 _____	6 _____	6 _____

[1] struggle [ˈstrʌgl] *Schwierigkeiten haben* [2] artificial [ˌɑːtɪˈfɪʃəl] *künstlich* [3] exchange [ɪksˈtʃeɪndʒ] *Austausch*

18 A trip to Greenwich (Will-future)

When Onno and the Wright family arrive at Greenwich market, things seem to get a little bit out of control. The children have very spontaneous[1] and adventurous ideas. Use the *will-future* in order to complete the statements.

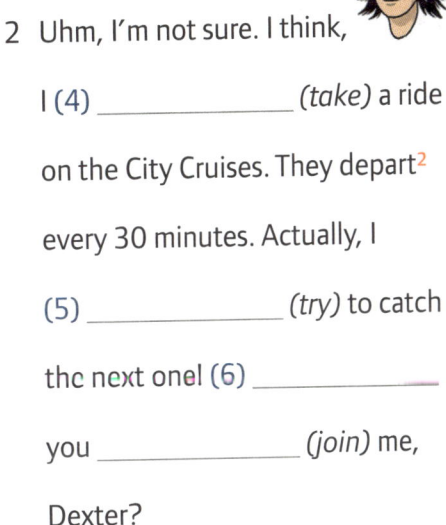

1 This place is just right for me!

First of all, I (1) _____

(buy) myself new sunglasses and

then I (2) _____ *(go)*

for some new shoes. Kayla,

(3) _____ you

_____ *(come)* with me?

2 Uhm, I'm not sure. I think,

I (4) _____ *(take)* a ride

on the City Cruises. They depart[2]

every 30 minutes. Actually, I

(5) _____ *(try)* to catch

the next one! (6) _____

you _____ *(join)* me,

Dexter?

3 That sounds so boring!

I (7) _____ *(fly)* a real Airbus at

the airplane[3] simulator centre! You can

take a 30-minute session in an Airbus

A380 or a different airplane. Yes, I (8)

_____ *(do)* it! Mum? Dad!?

4 I am fine with everything …

Although, I need some things for

school! I (9) _____ *(go)*

to a shop if you don't mind. After

that, I (10) _____ *(join)*

Dexter at the airplane centre! OK?

[1] spontaneous [spɒnˈteɪniəs] *spontan*   [2] depart [dɪˈpɑːt] *hier: ablegen*   [3] airplane [ˈeəpleɪn] *Flugzeug*

19 Excursion: In the country – out of town

Are you a country girl or a country boy?
Answer the questions and see how many
out-of-town words you know.

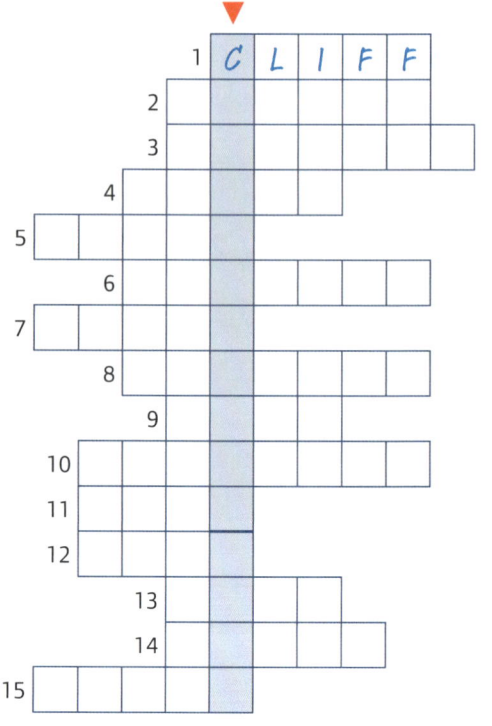

1   A high area of rock, often by the sea
    or the coast, not good to fall off.

2   A big … with lots of trees.

3   Country kids usually like … activities. They
    don't like to be in the house too much.

4   Not a river, but something like it, built
    by men.

5   There are lovely beaches on the English …

6   Not near / not close.

7   It's not the best for cycling. It's up and
    down, it's very …

8   If you get hungry in the countryside,
    just go …

9   City kids use sightseeing busses. Country
    kids simply go on a … tour in order to
    explore the area.

10 In city life, you find cars and shops.
    In …, you see wild animals and plants.

11 In a town, you swim in a swimming
    pool, in the country, you can swim
    in a …

12 Country kids don't sleep in a hotel
    but in a …

13 You can use paddles or an engine in
    order to move a … from A to B.

14 Not a noisy town, but a … village.

15 There are lots of fish in this …
    because the water is very clean.

Use the letters in the blue boxes in order to complete the sentence.

If you are sick and tired of city life, just pack your bags and make a

_____   _____ !

20 I'll do it (Will-future)

Look at the pictures and the sentences. What could your spontaneous reaction be?
Unscramble[1] the words in the box and use them to write your answer.

Buddy is hungry.

OK, I'll feed him.

I've lost my teddy.

_____

I couldn't hear you.

_____

phel •
deef ✔ •
difn •
ysa ainga •
nurt fof •
ehva …

The music is too loud.

_____

What can I get you?

_____

I can't do this.

_____

21 Lots of questions

Some English words have no plural form and are followed by a singular verb form. There
are nine of these in this box. Underline them. Then complete Dexter's questions to Onno
with some of the words from the box. Add the correct verb form when it is needed.

> trousers • hair • cupboard • France • homework • rain • money •
> zoo • furniture • vegetable • information • maths • life ✔

1 _____ my favourite subject. What's yours, Onno?

2 Onno, do you have to do a lot of _____ after school?

3 How often do you wash your _____ , Onno? Every day, like me?

4 Your _____ really cool. Where did you get them?

5 Onno, do you know a good website where I can get some _____

about the European Union? I need it for a presentation.

[1] unscramble [ʌnˈskræmbl] *in die richtige Reihenfolge bringen*

22 School time 🗋

a) Read the four text parts and put them in the right order. Write numbers 1 to 4 in the boxes.

☐ It was Onno's third day at the school and he had no problem finding his classroom again. His twin sister Merit was already there. She was laughing and chatting away with Pierre and three other boys. Onno found it quite unfair that his sister always had lots of people around her. Why didn't he? 'Hi brother,' Merit shouted across the room. 'How's life?' Onno didn't know how to answer this complex[1] question, so he simply said 'hi' and slowly walked over to Merit and the boys.

☐ 'I'll be with you in a minute,' Mr Wright shouted from the house. Onno nodded – even after a few days in England he still liked body language better than real language. He was waiting outside in front of the garage, next to the Wrights' car. Mr Wright was taking Onno to Roehampton College this morning so that he wouldn't get lost. (Not again.) Quite a nice thing, this big family car, Onno thought. Compared to the shower in the house, for example. Again this morning, Onno had had the greatest trouble with the shower in the Wrights' bathroom. He just couldn't get any hot water out of it, only cold – and he felt too stupid to ask. Thirteen years old and not able to make a shower work? No! Better to stand under cold water. 'Are you going to drive this morning?' Mr Wright said as he was coming towards the car. Onno looked at him, puzzled. 'You're at the wrong door, my friend,' Mr Wright explained. 'We drive on the left in this country.' Onno felt like an idiot as he was walking round the car and getting into the passenger seat.

☐ A few minutes later one of the college teachers came in. 'Good morning everybody. Now, today I'm going to give you the results of the tests you did two days ago. And on the basis of the tests, you will be put in different groups.' A big smile appeared on Onno's face when he got his results. They were good, very good! Better than Merit's. And – the best thing – he was going into a different group from her. Together with Carlos and Nevio, two boys who seemed to be very friendly. The day began to look brighter for Onno.

---

[1] complex ['kɒmpleks] *schwierig*

'I'm taking you through Richmond Park today,' Mr Wright said. 'It's one of the largest parks in London and in fact in Europe. If you're lucky, you can even see deer here.' 'Really?' Onno looked around. He couldn't see any deer. Well, it was probably a bit too early for them – half past eight in the morning. What a silly idea to go to school during the holidays. 'Has Mrs Wright talked to you about the trip we want to make to Greenwich next week?' Mr Wright asked, looking at Onno. Onno nodded but he had no idea what he meant. It soon became clear. 'In Greenwich there's the zero meridian[1] that divides the world into east and west. You can stand over it and have one leg in the east and one leg in the west. It's only about 14 miles from here. – Ah, there's your college over there. I'll let you out here. Mrs Wright will come and pick you up this afternoon. Enjoy your day!'
'Thank you. Bye-bye.' Onno got out of the car, looked left and right and crossed the street. Big mistake! He hadn't realised that in England you first look right and then left because cars come from the other side. Well, he was lucky, but one driver was shouting angrily in his car.

b) **Mark** at least seven sentences or parts of sentences that tell you something about Onno's feelings and his inner world. Example:

'I'll be with you in a minute,' Mr Wright shouted from the house. Onno nodded – even after a few days in England he still liked body language better than real language. He was

c) What do these numbers stand for in the text?

3	*It is Onno's third day at school.*
14	
13	
0	

23 Sports

Odd[2] word out: which of the four words is different? **Mark** one word in each line.

1 pitch – court[3] – ball – stadium

2 semi-final – final – half-pipe[4] – halftime

3 goalkeeper – referee – adult – coach

4 penalty[5] – basket – goal – shot

5 hit – beat – play – spot

6 competition – trainers – racket[6] – helmet

---

[1] zero meridian [ˈzɪərəʊ məˈrɪdɪən] *Nullmeridian*   [2] odd [ɒd] *hier: unpassend*   [3] court [kɔːt] *hier: Sportplatz*
[4] half-pipe [ˈhalf-paɪp] *Rampe*   [5] penalty [ˈpenəlti] *Strafe*   [6] racket [ˈrækɪt] *Schläger (Sport)*

24 Excursion: A quiz on Scotland 🎧

You can take part in this quiz, which was given at Junior Language College Roehampton. Listen to the 14 questions and <mark>mark</mark> the correct answers.

1 [A] on Burns Night   [B] for birthdays   [C] on December 31st

2 [A] Princes Street   [B] Holyrood Palace   [C] Arthur's Seat

3[1] [A] a Scottish uniform [B] a kind of skirt   [C] a special Scottish hat

4 [A] old   [B] pretty   [C] bad

5 [A] Aberdeen   [B] Dundee   [C] Glasgow

6[2] [A] John Logie Baird   [B] Alexander Fleming   [C] Alexander Bell

7 [A] Scotland   [B] Hoy   [C] the biggest of the Orkney Islands

8 [A] Loch Ness   [B] Loch Lomond   [C] Loch Tay

9 [A] Glasgow   [B] Aberdeen   [C] Edinburgh

10 [A] a great Scottish hero [B] a famous whisky   [C] the highest mountain in Scotland

11 [A] octopus   [B] salmon[3]   [C] herring[4]

12 [A] Edinburgh   [B] Glasgow   [C] Aberdeen

13[5] [A] St Andrew   [B] St George   [C] St David

14 [A] ouch, it hurts   [B] yes   [C] hello

[1] kilt [kɪlt] *Schottenrock*   [2] inventor [ɪnˈventə(r)] *Erfinder*   [3] salmon [ˈsæmən] *Lachs*   [4] herring [ˈherɪŋ] *Hering*
[5] patron saint [ˈpeɪtrən seɪnt] *Schutzheiliger*

25 At the Language College (Relative clauses, contact clauses)

a) Here are some things Merit and Onno have found out after a few days at the college. Read the following sentences. If you can leave out the relative pronoun *which* or *who*, put it in brackets ( ).

1 Katrina Reid, the Scottish teacher, is the one (who) they both like best.

2 In the morning break, which starts at 10.30, you can have tea, coffee or hot chocolate.

3 Everybody who comes to class late must read out a poem to the whole class.

4 Listening to real radio news during the lessons is something which Onno really enjoys.

5 The best place for a pizza during lunch break is the takeaway which is around the corner from the Language College in Radcliffe Road.

6 There is one boy who Merit seems to like – they hang out together in every break.

b) Here is more information about the Language College and the summer course. Complete the text with *who, that* or *which*. Put them in brackets ( ) if you can leave them out.

1 Singing songs at the beginning of the lesson is something _(which)_ most of the students find childish.

2 Pedro is another student in the course _____ comes from Madrid, Spain.

3 Katrina Reid is the only teacher on the summer course _____ comes to the college by bike.

4 Roehampton Junior Language College is the only college in the south-west of London _____ offers summer courses for teenagers.

5 The times _____ most students enjoy a lot are the breaks when people talk and have fun together.

6 There is one teacher _____ most students don't like very much. His jokes are so boring!

7 The project work _____ most teenagers choose is 'The London Underground'.

8 English is the only language _____ is allowed during lessons.

26 Opposites

How about a game of dominoes? Put the domino blocks in the right order. The first domino is the one with 'Start' on it – that's number 7. On the yellow side of the domino you'll see the expression 'wake up'. Find the domino that has the opposite meaning of 'wake up' on blue. That's number 3 with 'fall asleep'. So write '3' after number 7 on the line below. Do this until you get to the last domino, with 'Finish[1]' on it.

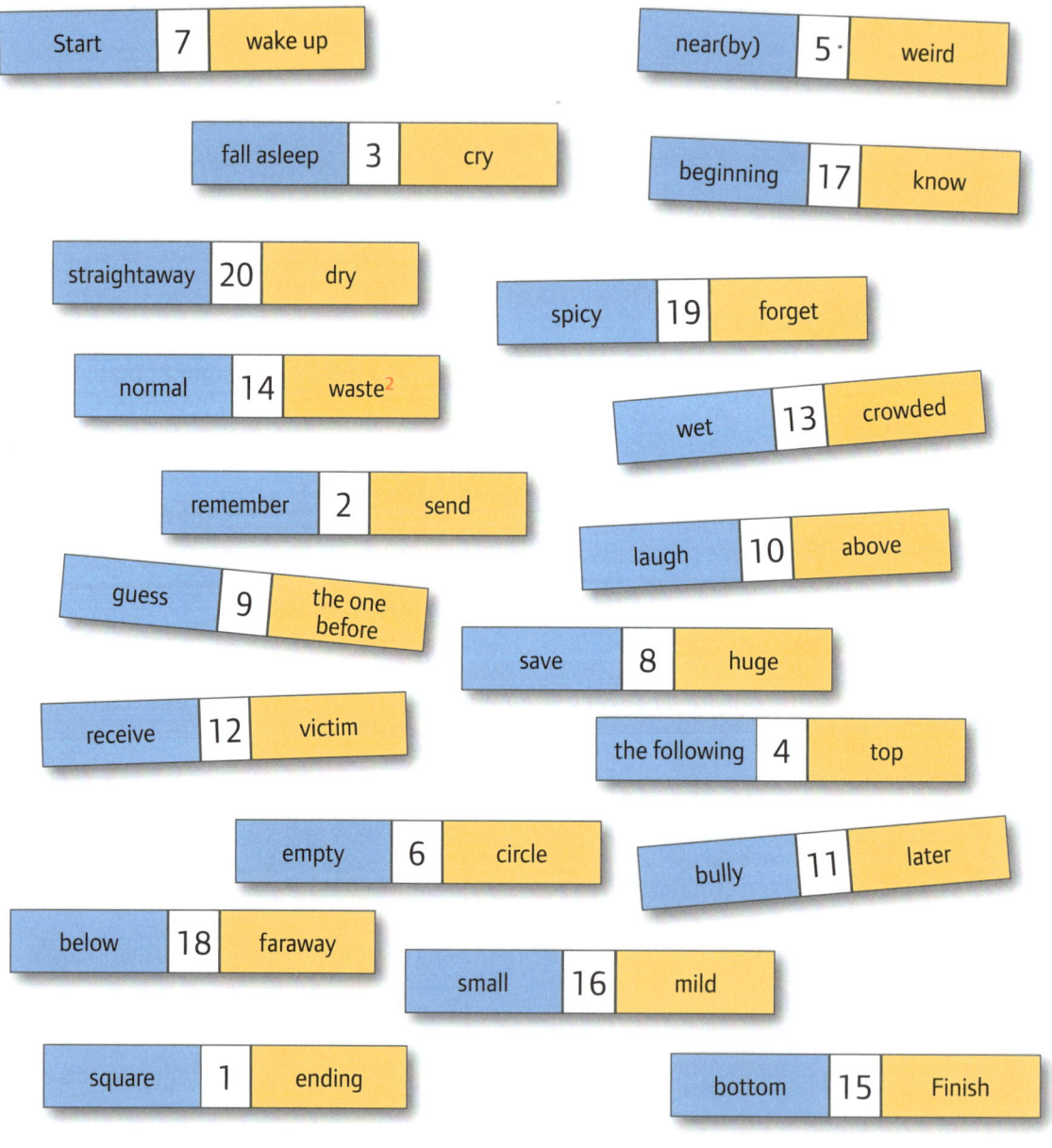

Start	7	wake up
near(by)	5 ·	weird
fall asleep	3	cry
beginning	17	know
straightaway	20	dry
spicy	19	forget
normal	14	waste[2]
wet	13	crowded
remember	2	send
laugh	10	above
guess	9	the one before
save	8	huge
receive	12	victim
the following	4	top
empty	6	circle
bully	11	later
below	18	faraway
small	16	mild
square	1	ending
bottom	15	Finish

7 –

---

[1] finish ['fınıʃ] *hier:* Ende   [2] waste [weɪst] *verschwenden*

27 What if? (Conditional II)

Complete each question (a) with the help of the picture and the verb next to it. Then use your own ideas in order to write an answer (b).

1 a) What would you do if *a snake came into* your house?

   b) I _____ .

come into

2 a) What would Onno do if Mrs Wright _____ him a fish burger?

   b) He _____ .

give

3 a) What would Merit do if her _____

   _____ ?

   b) She _____ .

fall into

4 a) What would Macy do if she _____ in the Wrights' house?

   b) She _____ .

see

5 a) What would Onno do if Grandma Wright _____ in front of the TV?

   b) I think he _____ .

fall asleep

6 a) What would Kayla do if her new boyfriend _____ her?

   b) I'm sure she _____ .

leave

7 a) What would Mrs Richardson say if Jessie

   _____ to have another teddy?

   b) She _____ .

want

28 How do you feel?

There are four groups of words here which describe feelings. Arrange the words on the stairs from weaker[1] to stronger, from positive to negative or the other way round. Some letters are already there in code. Break the code with the 'Have fun with this!' sentence. Write down the words. The words next to the stairs may help you.

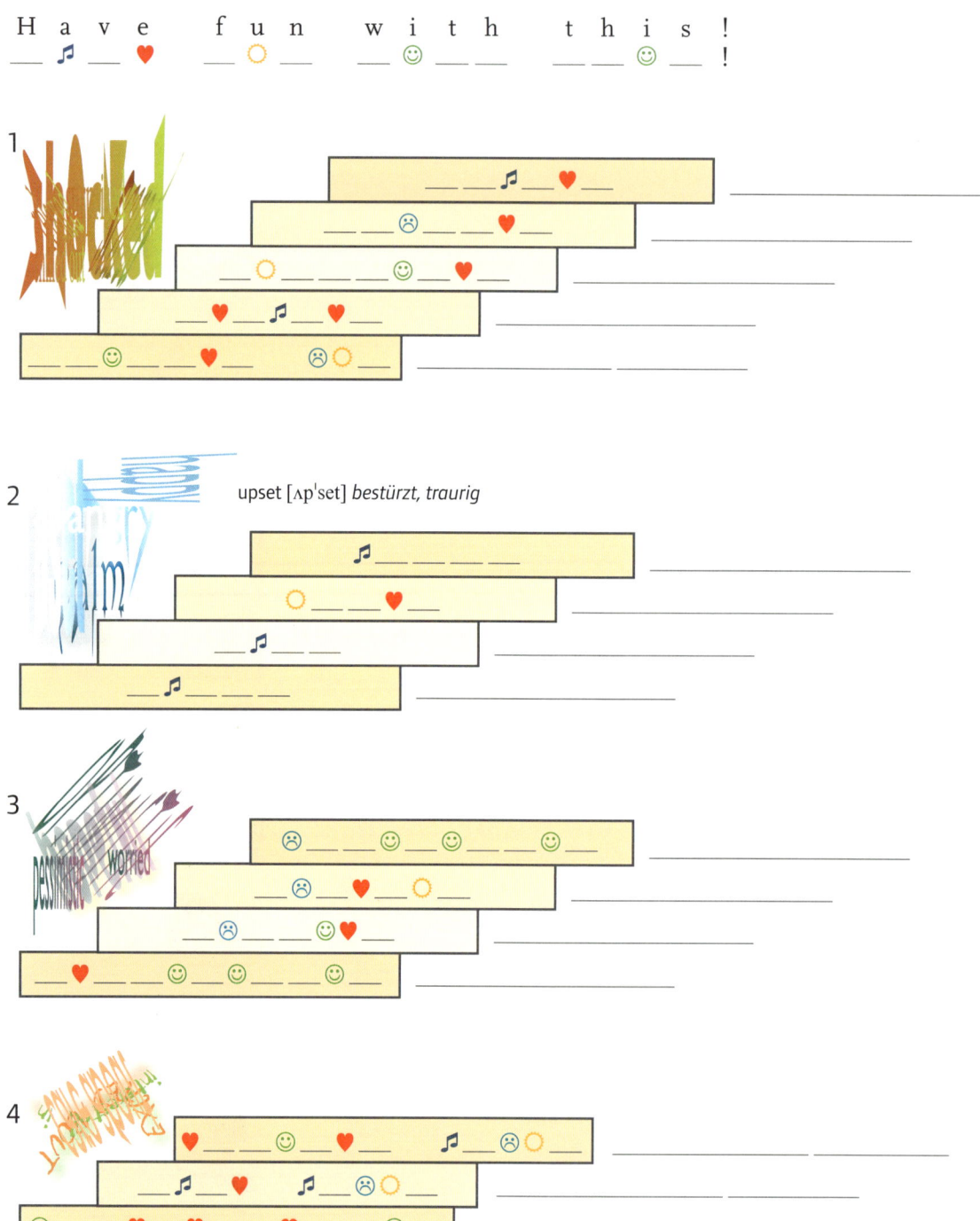

2 upset [ʌpˈset] *bestürzt, traurig*

[1] weak [wiːk] *schwach*

29 Youth Radio 99.9 🎧

a) 🖐 Onno's alarm clock in the Wrights' house is a radio. So, he often wakes up with the news on Youth Radio 99.9, a local radio station. Listen to this morning's headlines[1]. What do the news readers talk about? Tick (✔) *Yes* or *No*.

	Yes	No			Yes	No
1 music				5 traffic		
2 weather				6 film		
3 theatre				7 accident[2]		
4 sport				8 shopping		

b) 🖐 **Did you understand some of the details in the news? Mark the correct letter. Listen again, if necessary.**

1 The news readers' names are

  A Jessica and Scott. B Jennifer and Connor.

  C Jodie and Tyler.

2 A Spanish tourist is recovering[3] from an accident in London Bridge Hospital. Where did the accident happen?

  A At London Bridge B At Tower Bridge C At Millennium Bridge

3 What's the name of the man who fell into the Thames?

  A Alfonso B Not in the news C Javier

4 The new film 'Sounds in the Dark' is about a

  A tennis star. B plane crash. C rock band.

5 The tennis player Emily Wilson, who won the world's most famous tennis tournament[4], is from

  A Canada. B the USA. C the UK.

6 Emily wants to spend a part of her Wimbledon prize money on

  A her own plane. B a new bike. C a flat in London.

7 Tomorrow the weather in London will be

  A better. B worse. C more or less the same as today.

---

[1] headline [hed laɪn] *Schlagzeile* [2] accident ['æksɪdənt] *Unfall* [3] recover [rɪ'kʌvə(r)] *sich erholen*
[4] tournament ['tɔːnəmənt] *Wettkampf*

30 Dinner at the Richardsons'

'MERIT, PIERRE!' Mr Richardson was calling from the kitchen, trying to be louder than his little one-year-old son, Pablo, who had just fallen over on the
5 kitchen floor and was crying his eyes out. 'COULD YOU LOOK AFTER PABLO FOR A MOMENT, PLEASE?' Merit and Pierre looked at each other. They were sitting at the dining table[1] in the small living room,
10 talking and waiting for their evening meal. 'What?' whispered Merit, pulling a face. 'Look after that crybaby?' (During her time with the Richardsons, Merit had learned quite a few new English words and
15 'crybaby' was one of them.) 'Ah, e's all right,' said Pierre. He went into the kitchen and came back with Pablo on his arm. The little boy had stopped crying and seemed to enjoy looking at the world from about
20 one metre above the floor. 'Mr Richardson says we'll ave dinner later,' Pierre told Merit. 'Somebody as phoned and ordered eight meals. They're very busy in the kitchen.' By now, both Pierre and Merit
25 had found out that Mrs Richardson had just started a private takeaway service, and every now and then, people would call up and order from an online menu. The problem was that Mrs Richardson found it
30 quite difficult and got very, very nervous when too many orders came in at the same time. Even angry. At least noisy! 'Oh dear,' Merit said. 'And what about our bowling session? Carlos and the others will be at
35 the bowling centre in half an hour.' 'They'll ave to wait,' Pierre answered. In the kitchen, Mr and Mrs Richardson were now throwing pots and pans around, or at least that's what it sounded like. Pierre had to
40 speak louder: 'What else can we do? We must eat. I'm ungry.' Usually, Merit loved to listen to everything Pierre said because he had such a sweet French accent – he was always dropping the 'h' at the beginning of words – and because he was 45 such a cool and nice guy anyway. But she didn't like what she had just heard. 'Let them wait? Are you joking[2]? We can't do that! This cooking job will take an hour, we know that. They won't have time for us 50 before that. I have some biscuits. We can have them.' Merit didn't like the food in England much, especially not the Cuban-style food she was getting at the Richardsons'. But she had discovered 55 these delicious chocolate biscuits a few days after she had arrived in Wimbledon and most of the time she was surviving on them alone. At this point, a huge fight started between Mr and Mrs Richardson 60 in the kitchen. They were shouting at each other so loudly that little Pablo began to cry again. His bigger sister, Jessie, was coming down the stairs in order to see what was going on. 'I'm hungry,' she said. 65 'Is dinner ready?' she asked. Pierre put little Pablo on the floor. 'Well, if there's any food ready in the kitchen, it'll be taken away very soon. Merit, get your biscuits. Give some of them to the kids, turn the TV 70 on for Jessie and then let's go to the bowling centre.' That's what they did and that evening Merit was surer[3] than ever that Pierre was her hero.

---

[1] dining table ['daɪnɪŋ 'teɪbl] *Esstisch*   [2] joke [dʒəʊk] *Witze machen*   [3] sure [ʃɔːr, ʃʊər] *sicher*

a) Read the text on the left. Pierre has a French accent and drops the letter 'h' at the beginning of words. Go through the text and put the missing letters back in.

b) Read the phrases below. Which part of the text does each phrase describe? Write down the line number(s). The phrases are not in the same order as in the text.

1	A noisy little monster? – No, thank you!	*lines 6–11*
2	Out at last!	
3	Ordering meals by phone.	
4	A very loud argument next door.	
5	A 'shouting match' between father and son.	
6	Living on sweet things.	
7	Not an easy job for a nervous person.	
8	Enjoying the better view.	
9	Flying objects in the kitchen!	

31 **What would you do if …?** (Conditional II)

Mrs Richardson is curious and asks Merit a few questions while they are preparing dinner for the family. Fill in the right form of the verbs.

Mrs Richardson: Merit, darling, may I ask you a question?

Would you tell me if you didn't like it here?

Merit: Of course, Mrs Richardson, but I enjoy the time with your family very

much! I don't know what I (1) _____ *(do)* if I (2) _____
(feel) uncomfortable. That would be horrible!

Mrs Richardson: I have seen that you get on with Pierre very well … What (3) _____

you _____ *(say)* if he (4) _____ *(ask)* you for a date?

Merit: Well, I'm not sure … I guess, I (5) _____ *(say)* "yes" if he

(6) _____ *(ask)* me out. [giggles] Please don't tell him!

Mrs Richardson: No worries, I guess, you (7) _____ *(be)* very angry if I

(8) _____ *(tell)* him.

32 News update (Passive: simple present, simple past)

The Wimbledon station of the Metropolitan Police in London is just updating its website with the latest news. Use the words in brackets ( ) in order to fill the gaps. Remember that police reports often use the passive because they can't give away too much information.

A new video of our dog support unit (1) _was published_ (publish[1]) on our website last week. The latest video in our popular 'Police Dog Academy' will show you how we train our dogs to find bombs and other explosives.

Two older people (2) _____ (attack) by a young man at the St George's Road car park last night.

He (3) _____ (describe) as a

Scotland Yard – headquarter of the Metropolitan Police in London

tall white man with long dark hair. Anyone with information

(4) _____ (ask) to contact us on 020 8721 4906 or call Scotland Yard –

headquarter of the Metropolitan Police in London Crimestoppers anonymously[2] on 0800

555 111. Seven-year-old Jessie R. from 62 Redlington Road in Wimbledon (5)

_____ (report) missing on Thursday. She (6)

_____ (find) in the teddy bear section of Hamleys department store

later that day and (7) _____ (bring) home to her parents. A car (8)

_____ (steal) from outside 32 Chestnut Street on Friday night. This

could be linked to a break-in in the same street that night. Some big stones

(9) _____ (throw) into the window of Jones' watch shop and watches

costing more than £ 10,000 (10) _____

_____ (take). If you have any

information, call 020 8721 4906 or email us at

DCBarns@met. police.co.uk.

[1] publish [ˈpʌblɪʃ] veröffentlichen
[2] anonymous [əˈnɒnɪməs] anonym

33 A picture puzzle

Work out each puzzle and write down the answers.

1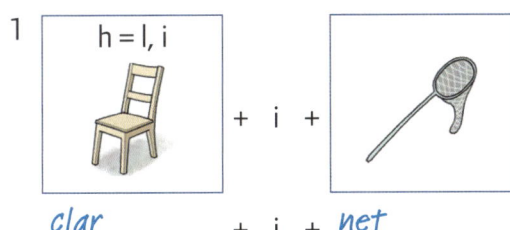

h = l, i

+ i +

clar_____ + i + net_____

= clarinet_____

2

a = e

+

_____ + _____

= _____

3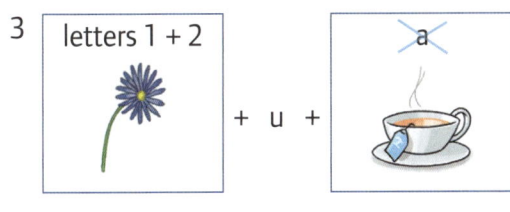

letters 1 + 2   a

+ u +

_____ + u + _____

= _____

4

+

_____ + _____

= _____

5

key   toise

+ i +

_____ + i + _____

= _____

6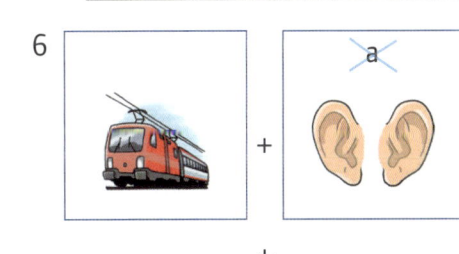

a

+

_____ + _____

= _____

7

letters 1 + 2   letters 1–3   + ation

+

_____ + _____

= _____

8

letters 2 + 5   o

v +   +

v + _____ + _____

= _____

9

letters 1 + 2   n = t

t +   + m +

t + _____ + m + _____

= _____

34 Before, after or at the same time? (Simple past, past perfect)

*When Merit was ready to take a photo
of Pierre, he left the room.*

*When Merit was ready to take a photo
of Pierre, he had left the room.*

Which sentence on the right fits the sentence on the left? Mark the right letter.

When Merit and Pierre arrived at the bowling centre, the others had started playing.	1	A Merit and Pierre were late for the first game.
		B Merit and Pierre were not late for the first game.
When Mrs Richardson finished her cooking job, Pablo fell asleep.	2	A Pablo fell asleep just after Mrs Richardson finished her job.
		B Pablo fell asleep while his mother was cooking.
Mr Richardson had left the kitchen when Mrs Richardson started cleaning the kitchen.	3	A Mr Richardson left the kitchen, and at the same time his wife started cleaning.
		B Mr Richardson was gone before Mrs Richardson started cleaning.
Jessie had turned off the TV when Mr Richardson looked into the living room.	4	A Mr Richardson saw Jessie when she was turning off the TV.
		B Mr Richardson didn't see Jessie turning off the TV.
When Merit and Pierre got home from their bowling session, they had finished all the chocolate biscuits.	5	A They ate the biscuits before they got home.
		B They ate the biscuits after they got home.
The bowling centre closed when Merit and Pierre and the others left at 9 pm.	6	A The bowling centre closed at 9 pm.
		B The bowling centre closed later than 9 pm.

35 Differences 🎧

Stress in similar German and English words is often different. **Mark** the stressed syllables in both languages. Then listen and check if you were right. What can you see?

	English 🇬🇧	German 🇩🇪	correct (✔) wrong (✗)		English 🇬🇧	German 🇩🇪	correct (✔) wrong (✗)
1	**ac**curate	akku**rat**		9	interested	interessiert	
2	appetite	Appetit		10	local	Lokal-	
3	biography	Biographie		11	million	Million	
4	contact	Kontakt		12	moment	Moment	
5	final	Finale		13	opera	Oper	
6	gallery	Galerie		14	personal	persönlich	
7	general	generell		15	talent	Talent	
8	industry	Industrie		16	traditional	traditionell	

36 Teach yourself a bit more English *(themselves, each other)*

Look at the pictures. Then complete the sentences. Decide if you need *themselves, each other* or no pronoun at all.

1 The two girls are _____ . *(take a photo of)*

2 The couple is _____ . *(shout at)*

3 These kids are _____ up. *(pull)*

4 'Let _____ at Victoria Station at 2.30 pm.' *(meet)*.

37 A phone call (Indirect speech)

Mrs Lehmann, Merit's mum, is on the phone with Mr Richardson. Here are some things they say.

1 I called Merit an hour ago.

2 Merit is still at the language school.

3 She sometimes forgets to take her mobile with her.

4 Can you tell her to call me back?

5 She will phone you tonight.

6 I miss Onno and Merit.

7 I'm sure they miss you too.

8 I will stay available. Bye for now!

After Merit comes back from the college later that day, Mr Richardson tells her about the phone call. Complete Mr Richardson's report.

1 Your mum said that she *had called you an hour before* .

2 I explained to her that you _____ .

3 I also said that you _____ .

4 Your mum then asked me if _____ .

5 I answered that _____ .

6 Your mum also said _____ .

7 I told her _____ .

8 And your mum said _____ .

38 British "dos and don'ts" (Modal verbs)

After Onno and Hannah have watched a TV programme on British culture, Onno has a few questions about the British "dos and don'ts". Fill in *can, may* or *must* (nicht müssen = *need not*, nicht dürfen = *must not*).

Onno: Uhm, there are quite many rules to stick to when you are around British people ...

Hannah: What do you mean? You (1) _____ (nicht müssen) stick to any rules!

Onno: For example, I (2) _____ (müssen) always stand in line, wherever I go.

Hannah: Well, I assume[1] that you do the same in Germany. Or (3) _____
             (dürfen) German people just pass others in order to get what they want?

Onno: Of course, not. However, (4) _____ (dürfen) I ask
             you a very personal question?

Hannah: Yes, you (5) _____ (dürfen). That was a very British way of
             introducing a question by the way. [giggles]

Onno: Do you always say things like "excuse me", "please", "thank you" or "sorry" when
              you talk other people?

Hannah: Uhm, actually... yes. For example, you (6) _____ (können) say

             "sorry" if someone bumps into you but you (7) _____ (müssen) say

             "sorry" when you bump into someone else. You (8) _____ (müssen)

             say "please" whenever you ask for something but you (9) _____

             (können) say "thank you" in many other ways. When you approach[2] a stranger,

             you (10) _____ (müssen) say "excuse me" before you talk. When

             you talk to a friend, you (11) _____ (können) say whatever you

             like, as long as it is polite.

Onno: Ok, excuse me, darling, I am very, very sorry but (12) _____
             (können) I please, please eat your desert today? Thank you soooo ... much in
             advance[3]! [giggles]

Hannah: It's "may". "May I eat your desert today?"! Hmmpf... [grumbles]

---

[1] assume [əˈsjuːm] *annehmen*   [2] approach [əˈprəʊtʃ] *hier: Kontakt aufnehmen*   [3] in advance [ɪn ədˈvɑːn(t)s] *im Voraus*

39 Excursion: Across Canada by train 🎧

a) 📢 You have been invited to an information evening about a famous train journey through Canada's beautiful scenery[1]. Listen to the person giving information about the fascinating[2] railway trip. While you are listening, put the city names in the order in which they appear on the route.

_____ **Winnipeg**

_____ **Edmonton**

_____ **Sudbury**

_____ **Vancouver**

_____ **Saskatoon**

_____ **Sioux Lookout**

_1_ **Toronto**

_____ **Kamloops**

_____ **Jasper**

b) Answer the following questions by marking the right letter:

1 Will the train go through any French-speaking province?

  A Yes   B No

2 When was the 'Canadian' built?

  A 13 to 25 years ago   B 25 to 50 years ago   C More than 50 years ago

3 How many kilometres does the 'Canadian' travel on its way through Canada?

  A 4000 km   B 4500 km   C 5400 km

4 Where can you find Canada's prairies[3]?

  A beyond[4] Toronto   B beyond Vancouver   C beyond Winnipeg

---

[1] scenery ['siːnəri] _hier: Landschaft_   [2] fascinating ['fæsɪneɪtɪŋ] _faszinierend_   [3] prairie ['preəri] _Prärie, Grasebene_
[4] beyond [bi'ɒnd] _jenseits von_

40 A final chat with Mrs Reid (Modal substitutes)

It's the last day at the college and Merit, Onno and a boy called Pedro are having a chat with one of their teachers about the course and their stay in England.
Complete the dialogue with the correct forms of *be able to*, *be allowed to* and *have to*.

> 'll be able to · won't be allowed to · won't have to · wasn't able to ✔ ·
> was allowed to · had to · 'll have to · didn't have to

Mrs Reid: So, do you think your English has improved in the last four weeks?

Merit: Oh yes! When I arrived here, I (1) _wasn't able to_ understand anybody in my
host family.

Onno: And I (2) _____ look up lots of
English words on my smartphone at the beginning.

Pedro: I (3) _____ speak much English with my
host family because we just watched TV all the time!

Mrs Reid: Oh! Well, that's interesting. But maybe you learned things from television too.
And did you enjoy your time here in London?

Onno: Yes, I did. I (4) _____ stay up until
midnight every night and hang out with Dexter.

Mrs Reid: That sounds great! I'm sure you (5) _____
do that back in Germany after school has started again.

Merit: I'm afraid you're right. We (6) _____ get up at
6.30 in the morning for school.

Pedro: 6.30? Crazy Germans! I (7) _____ sleep until
8 o'clock. How about you, Mrs Reid? When do you get up in the morning?

Mrs Reid: Well, I'm lucky. My holidays start after this course is over, and I (8) _____

_____ get up early for another three weeks.

Merit: I'll miss you, Mrs Reid!

41 Gatwick Airport 🗎

'G! Your turn.' Dexter looked at Onno. 'Can't you think of a city with G?' 'Just wait,' Onno grumbled, going through hundreds of cities in his head, but strangely, not a single one of them started with the letter G. 'G, G, G? Ah, I've got it: Greenwich!' he shouted proudly. 'Greenwich? Come on, Onno, Greenwich is not a city, it's a district[1] of London,' Dexter protested. 'OK, Geilenkirchen then. A town in Germany. Not too far from Aachen. H. Your turn,' Onno said, looking very happy that he had thought of this place. He was feeling quite good this afternoon anyway. After three long weeks, the day had finally come when he was allowed to go home again, back to Hamburg. Although … in a way, after the first shocking days, it hadn't been so bad. He had met some very OK people, like Carlos and Nevio at the college; and Dexter had become a really good friend. They had a lot of fun playing games together, lots of card games or the alphabet game they were playing now. This alphabet game was good because you could play it anywhere[2], even here at Gatwick Airport in front of the check-in desk.

Merit was following Mr Richardson through the door into the South Terminal of Gatwick Airport. She felt bad, terrible, really awful. Her bag weighed almost more than her – with all those chocolate biscuits she was taking home. Pablo, in his father's arms, was watching her all the time with a big lolly in his mouth, and Pierre hadn't had time to come to the airport with her in order to say goodbye! He was getting ready for his train journey back to Paris and Orléans later today. Boys! If she was Pierre, she would have packed earlier and she would have had time to go to the airport with a … a very special friend. Or maybe he didn't feel that way … about her? But he said he did. And he promised that he would write to her. Merit felt that something in the middle of her body, probably her heart, was beginning to get bigger and bigger and weigh more and more. 'Hi, sister! Do you know a city starting with Q?' Onno asked when she got close. (He didn't even realise he was speaking English to her!) 'No,' she said, with a dreamy look in her eyes and a strangely monotone[3] voice. 'Quebec.' 'Wow,' Onno was excited. 'Quebec! Now R. Your turn, Dexter.' Mrs Wright, who had taken Onno to the airport, and Mr Richardson said hello to each other and then goodbye because he had to help his wife at home and take Pierre to St Pancras Station in London. He could leave now that Merit was with her brother and Mrs Wright. 'So, Merit, I hope you have had a good time with us. Goodbye then and take care. Byebye.' Merit watched him going towards the exit. Little Pablo was reaching high into the air with his lolly, trying to say goodbye, and Merit felt another big thing in her body, this time in her throat. 'Let's move to the gate,' Mrs Wright said. 'It's time.'

On the plane, Merit is writing an email to Pierre. Onno is writing one to Dexter. Write down at least five sentences for each email.

[1] district ['dɪstrɪkt] *Bezirk* [2] anywhere ['eniweə(r)] *irgendwo* [3] monotone ['mɒnətəʊn] *eintönig*

1 This is England! 📄

a) 1 Mrs Wright · 2 Dexter · 3 Onno · 4 Kayla
5 Hannah · 6 Macy · 7 Grandma Wright

b)

	Right	Wrong	Not in the text
1	H	M	F
2	A	C	R
3	U	N	L
4	A	W	O
5	D	H	V
6	L	E	B
7	G	R	O

Onno is from **HAMBURG**.

2 It's a dog's life!

1 appetite
2 meat
3 spicy
4 mild
5 takeaway
6 dishes
7 sauces
8 uncooked
9 salmon
10 vegetables
11 lentils
12 allergic

3 Talking about transport

a) 1 **walk** to school / to the bus stop / home
2 **change to** the Northern Line / platform 7 / the underground
3 **take** the bus / the underground / a ride / a taxi
4 **go by** car / taxi / bike / plane / boat
5 **get off** the train / the bus / at the next stop / here / your bike
6 **arrive at** work / the airport / the station / school / a friend's house

b) **One word:** sightseeing · airport · underground · northbound · Travelcard
Two words: rush hour · bus stop · ticket machine · bike tour · speed limit · city centre (bus tour, city tour, ticket centre)

4 An email for Onno

1 got
2 told
3 Have … been
4 've/have never been
5 went
6 've/have had
7 moved
8 've/have already been
9 played
10 beat

5 Asking the way 🎧

a) 1 S · 2 H · 3 E · 4 E · 5 N

It's **Sheen** Road.

b)

5	Walk along Red Lion Street for a few minutes, and the Odeon is on the left side of the street.
4	At the end of Eton Street, turn ~~left~~ right into Red Lion Street.
1	Well, first of all you walk down Evelyn Road till you come to George Street.
3	Turn left into Eton Street.
2	Turn right there, go along George Street, past the big shopping mall.

6 Some facts about the Wright family

1 Mrs Wright sang in the Richmond Choir last summer.
2 Mr Wright has worked as a pilot for 15 years.
3 Mrs and Mr Wright have been married since June 23rd, 1994.
4 Hannah Wright has been on Facebook since her 15th birthday.
5 Dexter Wright has kept a diary for six months.
6 Kayla Wright dated her boyfriend Ben last week.
7 Grandma Wright has lived in Richmond for 45 years.
8 Macy caught three mice last April.

7 Oh! Ouch! The sounds [əʊ] and [aʊ] 🎧

1 around the table
2 the house in Richmond
3 cool sound
4 you know
5 foul play
6 below zero
7 a sore throat
8 a cold shower
9 Oh no!
10 touch ground
11 not now
12 south-west London
13 our own clothes
14 loud laughter

8 What has been happening?

1 The dog has been sleeping for two hours / … since 9 pm.

2 She has been watching (her favourite programme on) TV for half an hour … / … since 10.30.

3 Kayla has been talking (to her best friend) on the phone for two and a half hours. /… since 8.30.

4 Hannah has been doing her hair for one hour. / … since 10 o'clock.

5 Grandma has been doing a crossword puzzle (in the armchair) for one and a half hours. /… since 9.30.

6 Dexter has been listening to his MP3 player for one hour and 15 minutes. /… since 9.45.

7 Mr Wright has been flying across the Atlantic for three hours. /… since 8 o'clock.

9 Wimbledon – here I am 🗋

1 Merit is staying with a family in Wimbledon.

2 She has 748 friends on a (famous) social networking service.

3 She must improve her English, her parents say.

4 She came to England/London by plane.

5 She has one of the rooms under the roof.

6 She isn't a shy girl.

7 She is puzzled because she doesn't know who the little girl is.

8 She seems to like Pierre.

10 If A, then B

1 'll get

2 gets

3 will be

4 's/is

5 won't / will not grumble

6 doesn't / does not grumble

7 won't / will not have

8 doesn't / does not have

9 'll / will be

10 's/is

11 will come and visit

11 In town

1 STADIUM

2 CAPITAL

3 CAR PARK

4 CIRCUS

5 COLUMN

6 MOSQUE

7 PARLIAMENT

8 SQUARE

9 COMMUNITY HALL

10 SHOPPING MALL

> IF YOU ARE TIRED OF LONDON, YOU ARE TIRED OF LIFE.

12 A trip to the Science Museum

Box: words for 'and':
12 – although · 4 – because · 5 – but · 6 – so · 10 (4) – when · 9 – where

Box: words for 'nice':
2 – 40-minute · 11 – best · 1 – famous · 3 (7/8) – impressive · 8 (3) – large · 7 (3/11) – old

Right order: 1 famous · 2 40-minute · 3 impressive · 4 because · 5 but · 6 so · 7 old · 8 large · 9 where · 10 when · 11 best · 12 although

> **APOLLO** (In the museum there is the famous Apollo 10 capsule[1], one of the spaceships[2] that went all the way to the moon.)

[1] capsule [ˈkæpsjuːl] Kapsel [2] spaceship [peɪsʃɪp] Raumschiff

13 In and out of London – Guess What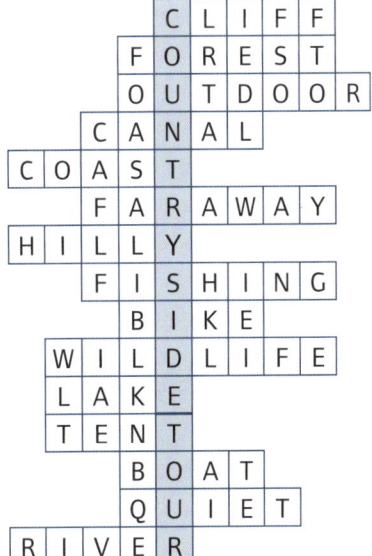

a) 1 K · 2 E · 3 C · 4 H · 5 A · 6 L ·
7 D · 8 I · 9 G · 10 B · 11 F · 12 J

b) Game 1: Photo 4 · Game 2: Photo 5
Game 3: Photo 1

14 Clever or unclever?

a) 1 happy/unhappy · 2 agree/disagree
3 friendly/unfriendly · 4 direct/indirect
5 clear/unclear · 6 regular/ irregular
7 sure/unsure · 8 possible/ impossible
9 cool/uncool · 10 appear/ disappear
10 tidy/untidy

b)

M	I	R	C	L	E	N	P	C
S	T	L	U	C	K	Y	N	O
N	E	X	E	L	Y	R	T	M
Y	E	S	N	E	I	N	I	F
F	O	P	L	V	M	R	E	O
A	S	O	W	E	S	H	O	R
I	M	P	O	R	T	A	N	T
R	E	U	N	E	P	P	S	A
S	I	L	U	T	R	P	N	B
N	S	A	F	E	M	Y	L	L
Y	E	R	T	C	T	N	S	E

1 unfair · 2 uncomfortable · 3 unhappy
4 unimportant · 5 unlucky · 6 unpopular
7 unclever · 8 unsafe

15 A college website

1 20 minutes
2 south-west
3 90 minutes
4 20 years
5 3
6 the UK
7 Learn English for Life!
8 He's the head teacher of the college.
9 at 3.30 pm
10 £1900 all-inclusive
11 Test your English
12 45 lessons

16 More about Merit

1 don't speak
2 will learn
3 will improve
4 take
5 will be able to
6 have
7 struggle
8 will ask
9 will learn
10 teaches

17 Stress in words

First syllable:
1 organise · 2 alphabet · 3 calendar
4 microphone · 5 parliament · 6 popular

Second syllable:
1 adventure · 2 biology · 3 exchange
4 musician · 5 photographer · 6 unfriendly

Third syllable:
1 information · 2 artificial · 3 conversation
4 electricity · 5 explanation · 6 unimportant

18 A trip to Greenwich

1 will buy · 2 will go · 3 will … come
4 will take · 5 will try · 6 will … join
7 will fly · 8 will do · 9 will go · 10 will join

19 Excursion: In the country – out of town

			C	L	I	F	F	
		F	O	R	E	S	T	
			O	U	T	D	O	O	R
		C	A	N	A	L		
	C	O	A	S	T			
		F	A	R	A	W	A	Y
H	I	L	L	Y				
		F	I	S	H	I	N	G
		B	I	K	E			
W	I	L	D	L	I	F	E	
L	A	K	E					
T	E	N	T					
		B	O	A	T			
		Q	U	I	E	T		
R	I	V	E	R				

If you are sick and tired of city life, just pack your bags and make a countryside tour!

Lösungen

20 I'll do it

1 OK, I'll feed him.
2 (OK,) I'll find it (for you).
3 (OK,) I'll say it again.
4 (OK,) I'll turn it off.
5 I'll have … (an orange juice / a cola /…).
6 (OK,) I'll help you.

21 Lots of questions

Words with no plural form:

hair · France · homework · rain · money · furniture · information · maths

1 Maths is
2 homework
3 hair
4 trousers are
5 information

22 School time 📄

a) 2 – 4 – 1 – 3

b) – even after a few days in England he still liked body language better than real language
– he felt too stupid to ask
– Onno looked at him, puzzled
– Onno felt like an idiot
– what a silly idea to go to school during the holidays
– he had no problem finding his classroom again
– Onno found it quite unfair that his sister always had lots of people around her
– Onno didn't know how to answer this complex question
– a big smile appeared on Onno's face

c) 3 It is Onno's third day at school.
14 It's 14 miles from Richmond to Greenwich.
13 Onno is 13 years old.
0 In Greenwich there's the zero meridian.

23 Sports

1 pitch, court, **ball**, stadium ('ball' isn't a location.)
2 semi-final, final, **half-pipe**, half-time (Only 'half-pipe' has nothing to do with team games.)
3 goalkeeper, referee, **adult**, coach (All except 'adult' have something to do with football.)
4 penalty, **basket**, goal, shot (All except 'basket' have something to do with football.)
5 hit, beat, play, **spot** (The first three verbs have something to do with sports.)
6 **competition**, trainers, racket, helmet (All except 'competition' are pieces of sports equipment.)

24 Excursion: A quiz on Scotland 🎧

1 C · 2 B · 3 B · 4 B · 5 A · 6 A · 7 C · 8 A · 9 C · 10 C · 11 B · 12 B · 13 A · 14 B

25 At the Language College

a) 1 Katrina Reid, the Scottish teacher, is the one (who) they both like best. · 4 Listening to real radio news during the lessons is something (which) Onno really enjoys. · 6 There is one boy (who) Merit seems to like – they hang out together in every break.

b) 1 (which/that)   5 (which/that)
2 who/that   6 (who/that)
3 who/that   7 (which/that)
4 which/that   8 which/that

26 Opposites

7 · 3 · 10 · 18 · 5 · 14 · 8 · 16 · 19 · 2 · 12 · 11 · 20 · 13 · 6 · 1 · 17 · 9 · 4 · 15

27 What if?

1a) a snake came into
 b) I would call the police. / (individual answer)
2a) gave
 b) He wouldn't eat it. / (individual answer)
3a) smartphone / mobile (phone) fell into the toilet
 b) She would cry out loud. / (individual answer)
4a) saw a thief
 b) She would run away. / (individual answer)
5a) fell asleep
 b) I think he would find a good programme and watch it. / (individual answer)
6a) left
 b) I'm sure she would find a new one. / (individual answer)
7a) wanted
 b) She would say 'Jessie, you've already got so many teddies!' / (individual answer)

28 How do you feel?

(jeweils von unten nach oben)
Stairs 1: chilled out · relaxed · surprised · shocked · scared
Stairs 2: happy · calm · upset · angry
Stairs 3: pessimistic · worried · hopeful · optimistic
Stairs 4: interested in · care about · excited about

29 Youth Radio 99.9 🎧

a) Yes: 2 · 4 · 6 · 7
 No: 1 · 3 · 5 · 8
b) 1 B · 2 C · 3 B · 4 B · 5 A
 6 C · 7 B

30 Dinner at the Richardsons' 🗋

a) line 15 – 'Ah, **h**e's all right …'
 line 21 – '… we'll **h**ave dinner later …'
 line 22 – 'Somebody **h**as phoned …'
 line 36 – 'They'll **h**ave to wait,'
 line 41 – 'I'm **h**ungry.'

b) 1 lines 6–11   6 lines 55–58
 2 lines 69–74   7 lines 28–32
 3 lines 22–28   8 lines 17–20
 4 lines 59–63   9 lines 36–39
 5 lines 1–3

31 What would you do if …?

1 would do · 2 felt · 3 would … say
4 asked · 5 would say · 6 asked
7 would be · 8 told

32 News update

1 was published   6 was found
2 were attacked   7 (was) brought
3 was described   8 was stolen
4 is asked   9 were thrown
5 was reported   10 were taken

33 A picture puzzle

1 c~~l~~la~~r~~ + i + n e t = clarinet
2 c a r + e~~x~~e r = career
3 fl~~ower~~ + u + te~~x~~ = flute
4 h e a d + p h o n e s = headphones
5 monk~~ey~~ + i + tor~~toise~~ = monitor
6 t r a i n + e~~x~~r s = trainers
7 pot~~ato~~ + pul~~lover~~ + a t i o n = population
8 v + ~~window~~ + li~~x~~n = violin
9 t + ru~~cksack~~ + m + pe~~x~~t = trumpet

34 Before, after or at the same time?

1 A · 2 A · 3 B · 4 B · 5 A · 6 A

35 Differences 🎧

	English	German
1	accurate	akkurat
2	appetite	Appetit
3	biography	Biographie
4	contact	Kontakt
5	final	Finale
6	gallery	Galerie
7	general	generell
8	industry	Industrie
9	interested	interessiert
10	local	Lokal-
11	million	Million
12	moment	Moment
13	opera	Oper
14	personal	persönlich
15	talent	Talent
16	traditional	traditionell

Most English words are stressed on the first syllable whereas most German words are stressed on the last syllable.

36 Teach yourself a bit more English

1. The two girls are taking a photo of themselves.
2. The couple is shouting at each other.
3. These kids are pulling themselves up.
4. 'Let's meet at Victoria Station at 2.30 pm.'

37 A phone call

1. Your mum said that she had called you an hour before.
2. I explained to her that you were still at the language school.
3. I also said that you sometimes forgot to take your mobile with you.
4. Your mum then asked me if I could tell you to call her back.
5. I answered that you would phone her tonight.
6. Your mum also said (that) she missed you and Onno.
7. I told her (that) I was sure you missed her too.
8. And your mum said (that) she would stay available.

38 British "dos and don'ts"

1 needn't · 2 must · 3 may · 4 may
5 may · 6 can · 7 must · 8 must · 9 can
10 must · 11 can · 12 (can)

39 Excursion:
Across Canada by train 🎧

a) Die Städtenamen von Osten nach Westen:
1 Toronto · 2 Sudbury · 3 Sioux Lookout
4 Winnipeg · 5 Saskatoon · 6 Edmonton
7 Jasper · 8 Kamloops · 9 Vancouver
b) 1 B · 2 C · 3 B · 4 C

40 A final chat with Mrs Reid

1 wasn't able to · 2 had to · 3 didn't have to / wasn't able to · 4 was allowed to · 5 won't be allowed to · 6 'll have to · 7 'll be able to · 8 won't have to

41 Gatwick Airport 📱

Hi Pierre,
I hope you got the train to Paris in time. You never know with Mr Richardson! That family is a bit crazy – but quite OK. I'm sitting on the plane and we will be landing in Hamburg soon. I don't want to go home! I really enjoyed my time in London. What about you? Shall we go back in the autumn holidays? If you ever want to come to Hamburg, you can stay with us. I'm sure my parents wouldn't have anything against it. Must stop writing now. Write back, pleeeease!

Lots of love ♥ ♥ ♥
Merit

Hi Dexter,
I'm still on the plane. Imagine, the pilot invited me to come into the cockpit!!! It was fantastic. Your dad has a super job. I tried to do the city alphabet with my sister. She couldn't even think of a city beginning with A. I don't think she was really interested. She's a bit strange today.
Come to Hamburg soon. And bring Macy!
CU
Onno